CBD Massage

The step-by-step guide to increase revenue in your Massage Therapy practice

Pamela Heavner

CBD Massage

The step-by-step guide to increase revenue in your Massage Therapy practice

Copyright 2021 by Pamela Heavner

For more information about Pamela Heavner and The Brand Bar Studio, please visit:

www.BrandBarStudio.com

FIRST EDITION

DEDICATION

To:

Tim, Rachel, Chad, Kaylee, and Alex,

For your love, patience, and support.

And

To Massage Therapists everywhere,

You make this world a much better place

Contents

Introduction

Since CBD[1] came onto the scene legally in 2018 there has been no shortage of companies calling my clinic trying sell me on their brand of CBD products. Their goal being to get me to carry, use, and sell their brand of CBD products to my clients. After my first experience with CBD topicals for pain, I knew there was something here that needed to be explored. Over the past few years, I have spent countless hours researching the science behind CBD, the legal constraints of its use, and how best to use CBD products in my practice. This is my attempt to gather and share with you the most pertinent information about adding CBD products and services into your massage therapy practice. My goal with this book is to share with you what I have discovered in a clear and concise manner and, hopefully, save you the tremendous amount of time and effort which I spent reading, interviewing experts, making phone calls, and attending conferences across the country. My hope is that it will provide you with

---

[1] Cannabidiol

a comprehensive resource for deciding if adding CBD products to your practice is right for you.

Because of the rising popularity of CBD products, one of the most common questions I get from my students and coaching clients is, "How can I incorporate CBD Massage and CBD products into my practice?" Realizing the need for detailed and clear information on how to incorporate CBD safely and legally into your practice, this book is meant to guide you step-by- step through how to educate yourself regarding CBD, specifically its use in massage, lay out a plan for incorporating CBD into your practice, then launching your new service and product line.

In this book I will only be addressing the use of CBD topicals in your practice. There is no question suggesting that your clients consume CBD in any other form is outside of your scope of practice as a massage therapist. This book is aimed at being a resource for you to determine if CBD topicals will be a legal, profitable, and beneficial addition to your practice.

CHAPTER ONE

The Basics

CBD products have become increasingly popular since the Agriculture Improvement Act of 2018, better known as the 2018 Farm Bill, was signed into law. CBD stores are popping up all over the country with an emphasis on selling a variety of tinctures, capsules, topicals, and creams to curious customers. As the popularity of CBD products has increased, it logically found its way into the massage therapy industry.

Many therapists have heard about the wonderful benefits of CBD and have considered incorporating it into their massage sessions. In my experience, the therapeutic benefits of massage therapy can be greatly enhanced by incorporating CBD products into your practice. Before you decide whether to carry CBD products and add them to your services menu, there are a few basics of cannabis that you need to know. I strongly believe you need to be educated on the products you are going to be offering to your clients. They will have a lot of questions about CBD and you are going to need to be prepared to guide them and to share appropriate information and resources about CBD products. For this reason, I start by sharing a lot of foundational information about CBD and some of the key terms related to CBD that you need to understand for yourself and your clients.

Cannabis, Hemp, and Marijuana

You may think that marijuana and hemp are two totally different plants. In fact, they are simply different names for the same type of plant. Cannabis is the official name for the genus of plant from which hemp and marijuana are derived. There are two main types of the cannabis plant: Indica and Sativa. The Sativa strain is typically perceived to provide an energizing effect that can help reduce stress and/or anxiety and increase focus and creativity. The Indica strain is typically perceived to provide pain relief, deep relaxation and to induce sleep.[2]

Hemp and marijuana are two of the various

---

[2] There is some scientific research that indicates that the perceived effects of Indica and Sativa is not consistent enough to generalize these distinctions

types of the *Cannabis sativa* plant. Both types contain CBD, but hemp contains a much higher percentage of CBD and an exceptionally low level of Tetrahydrocannabinol (THC) as compared to marijuana. In fact, industrial hemp, by definition, must have less than 0.3% of THC.[3]

To put it simply, marijuana is effectively defined[4] as a cannabis plant that contains more than 0.3 percent THC, and hemp is more narrowly defined as a cannabis plant that contains no more than 0.3 % of THC. However, remember that CBD can be obtained from both hemp and marijuana plants.

Cannabinoids

There are more than 100 various cannabinoids (compounds) in Cannabis. Cannabidiol (CBD) and Tetrahydrocannabinol (THC) are the two most widely discussed of these many cannabinoids. We are going to focus mostly on these two. While most people focus on the benefits of CBD when it comes to hemp extract, there are some other amazing compounds that can be found in the full or broad-spectrum product. Here are a few of the important others:

[3] As defined in Section 297A of the Agricultural Marketing Act of 1946 (AMA).
[4] The definition of marijuana in the Controlled Substances Act (21 U.S.C §§801 et. seq.) does not specify a THC threshold.

- **Cannabichromene (CBC):** Thought of as a complementary compound in relation to full-spectrum hemp. Has been shown to help with migraines. Typically found in low levels.

- **Cannabigerol (CBG):** Another key cannabinoid found in hemp, CBG works to fight pain, inflammation, and nausea.

- **Cannabinol (CBN):** has the potential to be a mildly psychoactive cannabinoid, however it is only found in trace amounts in Cannabis. This cannabinoid has also been shown to help regulate the immune system and works to relieve pain and inflammation caused by several conditions like arthritis.

- **Terpenes:** These are aromatic oils found in hemp and other plants that bind to receptors in the human body. They carry a wide variety of benefits. Terpenes play a part in the Entourage Effect that occurs in broad or full spectrum extracts.

- **Flavonoids:** are a group of phytonutrients (cannabinoids manufactured by plants) that serve as cell messengers. Flavonoids can also be readily found in vegetables and fruits.

Another term you may not be familiar with

is the *entourage effect.* This proposes that cannabis compounds work better when in combination with other cannabis compounds. They act synergistically with each other to improve the overall effects of the plant. Therefore, you may hear that CBD products work better when using a full or broad-spectrum product due to the entourage effect.

Full Spectrum, Broad Spectrum, and Isolate

When shopping for a reliable CBD product, you may come across several different terms with which you are not familiar. The marketing of CBD products is inundated with adjectives like *broad-spectrum, isolate,* and *full spectrum.* The main difference between these three terms correlates to the amount and variety of naturally occurring plant compounds in the extract. To help us to better understand these three terms, let's get to know the extraction process hemp undergoes a little bit better.

According to the Charlotte's Web blog article in their CBD 101 series, first cannabis plant material is reduced to a consistent size to prepare it for extraction, and the material is baked to decarboxylate the cannabinoids.[5]

[5] What Does Full-Spectrum Mean. (2018, August 29). Retrieved from charlottesweb. com: https://www.charlottesweb.com/blog/full-spectrum-cbd-oil)

"The reason that decarboxylation is necessary is because in their natural (raw) plant form, cannabinoids are not readily usable to the body's cannabinoid receptors. Both THC and CBD contain an acidic molecule and are in their inactive forms known as THCA and CBDA. These inactive forms are unable to bind with the cannabinoid receptors, and therefore will not produce the therapeutic effects a patient would expect."[6]

For this process to take place, two main mechanisms are required: time and heat. The next step in the process commonly utilizes either alcohol or Carbon Dioxide. Once finished, the newly sourced extract is diluted with a carrier oil.

For this CBD product to be considered "full-spectrum," it needs to be made up of all the various compounds found in hemp, including terpenes, flavonoids, and cannabinoids. If a product is labeled "broad-spectrum," it most likely contains more than a few compounds. By definition, broad spectrum extract should offer a minimum of 2 cannabinoids and one terpene. It may or may not contain THC. CBD "isolate" is extensively filtered and thoroughly processed so that it does not contain anything other than

[6] What is Decarboxylation. (n.d.). Retrieved from Aphria.ca: https://aphria.ca/blog/what-is-decarboxylation/

CBD. It does not contain any of the other plant compounds including THC.

Let's Review:

Full Spectrum: Made up of all the various compounds found in hemp such as terpenes, flavonoids, and cannabinoids. Full Spectrum does contain THC.

Broad Spectrum: Contains some of the compounds, but not all. Should possess a minimum of one terpene and two cannabinoids. Broad spectrum products may or may not contain THC.

Isolate: The CBD molecule is filtered and isolated so that only the CBD remains. Isolates do not contain any other plant compounds. Isolates do not contain THC.

The Endocanniniod System (ECS)

The endocannabinoid system (ECS) plays a very important role in the human body. This is due to its ability to play a crucial role in maintaining homeostasis, which encompasses the brain, immune, and endocrine system. It has a very wide scope of influence due to an abundance of cannabinoid receptors located anywhere from neurons to immune cells.

The three key components of the human endocannabinoid system are:

- **Cannabinoid receptors** found on the surface of cells;

- **Endocannabinoids** are small molecules that activate cannabinoid receptors; and

- **Metabolic enzymes** that break down endocannabinoids after they are used

Cannabinoid receptors

CB1 is one of the most abundant receptors in the central nervous system. It consists of 472 amino acids. These receptors are found at particularly high levels in the cerebellum, hippocampus, basal ganglia, neocortex, and brainstem.

CB2 consists of 360 amino acids. CB2 receptors occur mainly on immune cells. They are found all over the body, but they are highly concentrated in the peripheral nervous system, immune and digestive system, and organs: heart, eyes, kidneys, and lungs.

Endocannabinoids

Endocannabinoids are molecules that, like the plant cannabinoid CBD, bind to and activate cannabinoid receptors. There are two major endocannabinoids: anandamide and 2-AG. These two cannabinoids are made when needed on demand and used immediately. They are not made and stored for later.

Metabolic enzymes

The third part of the endocannabinoid triangle includes the metabolic enzymes that quickly destroy endocannabinoids within the ECS once they are used. We don't need to go into a deep dive into the types of enzymes.

Just remember, that the ECS has receptors that endocannabinoids and cannabinoids bind to and activate. These receptors have an influence over the entire body. Then the metabolic enzymes break down the endocannabinoids after they are used.

You now understand that the ECS acts as the master switchboard to help create balance throughout the body. There is barely a biological or physiological system in our bodies in which the endocannabinoids do not participate. Since the skin is the largest organ in the body, and it contains many cannabinoid receptors and endocannabinoids, the use of topical CBD oils and creams in massage therapy can enhance this multifaceted, homeostatic regulator in the body.

Let's Review

<u>Endocannabinoids:</u> Cannabinoids the body produces naturally.

<u>Phytocannabinoids:</u> Cannabinoids manufactured by plants.

<u>ECS:</u> The Endocannabinoid System plays a crucial role in maintaining the homeostasis of the human body.

CHAPTER TWO

Is it Legal?

To answer this question, we need to get to know the law on the federal and state level. On December 20th, 2018, the Agricultural Improvement Act, which you know better as the 2018 Farm Bill, was signed into law. This law legalized the production of hemp, which until then, had not been differentiated from other cannabis plants.

Before the Farm Bill, all types of cannabis, including hemp, were considered illegal under the 1970 Federal Controlled Substances Act. This legislation placed all cannabis as a Schedule 1 controlled substance, which defined cannabis as a material with no accepted medical benefits, a high potential for abuse, and an elevated likelihood for addiction.

The 2018 Farm Bill created a legal distinction between marijuana and hemp. By doing this, it removed some cannabis from the previous Schedule 1 status. Under the new legislation, hemp is classified as cannabis that contains less than 0.3% THC by weight, while marijuana is thus effectively limited to cannabis that contains more than 0.3% THC. Keep in mind that marijuana is still categorized as a Schedule 1 controlled substance. Therefore, CBD that is obtained from the marijuana plant (containing more than 0.3% THC) is still considered illegal under Federal law. Even though hemp is now considered an agricultural commodity, there are strict regulations governing how it is to be produced and sold. The Farm Bill gave the Food and Drug Administration (FDA) the power to regulate CBD's therapeutic claims, labeling, and appearance in drinks and foods. The United States Department of Agriculture (USDA) implements the other aspects of the Farm Bill. The slow pace of the USDA in issuing regulations has added to confusion at the state level. Because of the delay by the FDA, some states are waiting to adopt the parameters for the legal use of CBD products until there are clear Federal level guidelines in place to avoid conflicts between the two jurisdictions.

Even if CBD extract is sourced from hemp, it is still not legal in all 50 states. Not all states have adopted an unrestricted definition of hemp for their own Controlled Substances Acts (CSA). Until there is a change in the state's definition, hemp is still considered marijuana in these states.

To determine if you can legally use CBD sourced from hemp, you need to research the laws of the state in which you practice. A Google search of the legality of hemp in your state can provide you with a quick answer to the general laws governing its legality. There are also some remarkable websites out there that have diligently gathered information about the statue of each state's legislation that supports the use of hemp products.

As of the date of the publication of this book, Nebraska, Iowa, and Idaho have not legalized any type of CBD products within their jurisdiction. If you are a massage therapist in one of these three states, then the use of CBD topicals would not be legal in your practice. Be sure to stay up to date on changes to relevant legislation in your state. These laws could change at any moment.

In addition to understanding the Federal and state laws and regulations regarding hemp in your state, also look at any restrictions that may be in place in the county or city in which you practice. Generally, local governing bodies follow their state's restrictions. However, to protect yourself, review your local ordinances and/or reach out to your local jurisdiction and confirm the legality of industrial hemp-derived CBD products in your city or county.

CHAPTER THREE

Is CBD Massage Within My Scope of Practice?

Scope of practice laws are state-specific restrictions that determine what tasks massage therapists and other healthcare providers may undertake in the course of caring for clients. These restrictions can also be called standards of practice. They are typically outlined in the practice act which is administered by the governing board.

In the field of massage therapy, the scope of practice can vary widely from state to state. In fact, there are still 5 states[7] that have neither a defined scope of practice nor do they require a massage certification or license. With the wide disparity in standards, how can you find out if CBD topicals are within your scope of practice?

[7] Wyoming, Vermont, Oklahoma, Minnesota, and Kansas

To make this determination, start by determining the governing body for massage therapists in your state. Let's look at an example using my home state. In Virginia, massage therapy is regulated by the Virginia Board of Nursing. To determine what is in my scope of practice, I need to get this information directly from the resources provided by the regulating body. Most of this information can be found on their website[8]. Specifically find the area that addresses the laws and regulations for massage therapists. As an example, this is how the Virginia Code, as administered by the Virginia Board of Nursing, defines the scope of practice for massage therapy:

A "Massage therapist" means a person who meets the qualifications specified in this chapter and who is currently licensed by the Board. The practice of "Massage therapy" means the treatment of soft tissues for therapeutic purposes by the application of massage and bodywork techniques based on the manipulation or application of pressure to the muscular structure or soft tissues of the human body. The term "massage therapy" does not include the diagnosis or treatment of illness or disease or any service or procedure for which a license to practice medicine, nursing, midwifery, chiropractic, physical therapy, occupational therapy, acupuncture,

___
[8] https://www.dhp.virginia.gov/Boards/Nursing/

athletic training, or podiatry is required by law or any service described in § 54.1-3001(18).[9]

In addition to the definition of the duties of massage therapists, the Board addresses adding other modalities and services by stating in an additional guidance document:

> *Documentation of Training and Education:* *If modalities of bodywork and specialized massage are incorporated into massage therapy practice, the Board of Nursing recommends that the Licensed Massage Therapist (LMT) maintain documentation of education and/or training in that area.* [10]

This additional guidance (Documentation of Training and Education) on the scope of practice for massage therapists in Virginia, highlights an important topic: If a massage therapist is researching the boundaries of their scope of practice and find that the guidelines are vague and do not offer much assistance, consider getting a certificate of training in the proposed modality. When you are adding a new modality or service to your practice, you want to be certain you have the appropriate training and knowledge to safely provide that service. This allows you to

[9] Code of Virginia § 54.1-3000

[10] Virginia Board of Nursing Guidance document: 90-47

protect your client from any risk of injury and protect yourself from risk of liability. By pursuing a certificate of training, you will help ensure that you have the additional education and knowledge to keep your clients safe. If needed, a certificate of training can also make sure you are working within the boundaries of your scope by demonstrating to the governing body that you have the advanced training and education.

There are some states that have more detailed standards in place that may serve as a better roadmap. For example, let's look at the standards of practice issued by the state of North Carolina. Massage therapists in North Carolina are regulated by the North Carolina Board of Massage and Bodywork Therapy. Their website, www.bmbt.org, is packed with easy-to-read information that make access to important information readily available, including the Practice Act and Rules section. Although they do not list CBD specifically, they do directly address adding topical oils and creams to your massage:

The State clearly defined massage and bodywork therapy as:

Systems of activity applied to the soft tissues of the human body for therapeutic, educational, or relaxation purposes.

The application may include:

a. Pressure, friction, stroking, rocking, kneading, percussion, or passive or active stretching within the normal anatomical range of movement.

b. Complementary methods, including the external application of water, heat, cold, lubricants, and other topical preparations.

c. The use of mechanical devices that mimic or enhance actions that may possibly be done by the hands.[11]

This clearly outlines safe practices. As mentioned, it also specifically incorporates complimentary methods that include the external application of water, heat, cold, and lubricants; a clear reference to use of topicals as part of the provision of massage services.

Another great example of clearly stated scope of practice guidance is found in Nebraska. Their standards of practice are:

Massage Therapy means the physical, mechanical, or electrical manipulation of soft tissue for the therapeutic purposes of enhancing muscle relaxation, reducing stress, improving circulation, or instilling a greater sense of well-being and may include the use

---

[11] N.C. Gen. Stat. § 90-622(3)

of **oil**, salt glows, heat lamps, and hydrotherapy. Massage therapy does not include diagnosis or treatment or use of procedures for which a license to practice medicine or surgery, chiropractic, or podiatry is required nor the use of microwave diathermy, shortwave diathermy, ultrasound, transcutaneous electrical nerve stimulation, electrical stimulation of over thirty-five volts, neurological hyperstimulation, or spinal and joint adjustments. [12]

a. _Well-being_ includes, but is not limited to:

(1) Remediation, such as myofascial release, active/passive stretching, and similar modalities;

(2) Relaxation, such as Swedish Massage, hot stone, and similar modalities; and

(3) Holistic, such as Ortho-Bionomy®, polarity, shiatsu, reflexology, acupressure, and similar techniques.

b. _Mechanical or electrical manipulation_ includes, but is not limited to, the use of the following equipment:

(1) Electrical stimulation equipment under 35 volts output;

(2) Oscillating (vibrating) equipment; and

---

[12] Neb. Rev. Stat. § 38-1706 (Massage Therapy Practice Act)

(3) Hydrotherapy equipment.[13]

Again, in this example we see how topical oils are mentioned as being within the guidelines of a massage therapist's scope of practice. When states have a clearly defined standards of practice, massage therapists can feel confident knowing what they can safely and legally do and what practices they should avoid.

For practices in states without a clearly defined scope of practice, massage therapists can find themselves scratching their heads in confusion and endlessly looking for answers. If after reading your states standards of practice you still have questions about whether CBD topicals are allowed, I would suggest that you reach out directly to the governing board in the state in which you practice. In that correspondence, ask what their policies are when using CBD products in your practice. Be sure to mention that you only use topical CBD products that are sourced from legal industrial hemp. The information you obtain will help give you peace of mind in your consideration of adding CBD massage into your practice.

---

[13] 172 Neb. Admin. Code, Ch. 81 § 002.21

CHAPTER FOUR

Choosing a Product Line

As massage therapists, we understand how important it is to know what is in the products we are using on our clients. Every client comes to us with different tolerances and sensitivities. Our clients trust us to choose the products that are safest and most effective. For these reasons, it is always important to understand the complexity of the components of any topical oil or cream we use in our practice. This is true not only for a CBD product, but also for other topical products that are often used in our practices, like Biofreeze and essential oils. Therefore, getting to know the ingredients and additives in CBD products is crucial for good client care.

Here is a list of the most important factors to consider when choosing your CBD product line.

1. Know where the CBD is sourced

One important element of choosing the best CBD product is knowing where the product was grown and how it was extracted. Did you know that one of miraculous benefits of growing hemp is that it has been shown to help reduce soil toxicity? In fact, for over a decade, industrial hemp growing in the environs of the abandoned Chernobyl nuclear power plant in Pripyat, Ukraine has been helping to reduce soil toxicity. [14]

Why is this important? Because the hemp plants grown in this area remove the toxic materials from the ground and absorb them into their own system, transforming the plant into a toxic material that should not be consumed by anyone. The market is becoming flooded with cheap CBD products that have been sourced from environments like this which have the potential to be harmful to the user, rather than effective. Thus, it is vital to know where the hemp used in creating the CBD product is cultivated.

---

[14] *Why It's Important to Know the Source of Your CBD Products.* (2016, April 21). Retrieved from Pet.Releaf.com: https://petreleaf.com/blog/radio-active-or-toxic-cbd-know-your-source

2. Third Party Testing and COA

As it is with any product, you should reasonably be able to determine all of the ingredients of a CBD product. So, make sure the company you choose conducts rigorous third-party testing on every batch of its products — and make sure the results of those tests are readily available, preferably online. The information that is available from such testing is called a Certificate of Analysis (COA). The information contained in a COA helps to ensure that a manufacturer's products are made to certain specifications, including the quantity of cannabinoids found in each product. In addition to cannabinoids, this certificate should show details on the levels of heavy metals, pesticides, solvents, and THC found in an individual batch of the product that was tested. COAs are meant to keep customers safe and informed, but they also help verify the quality of the product.

Quality CBD products on the market will provide a batch or lot number on each products packaging. That batch number can be used to search the company's website and download the COA report for each batch. On one of the products I carry, the company has provided a QR code on each product to increase the ease of use in this verification process. The consumer can scan the QR code and see the COA for the exact product they are holding in their hand. It is quick and easy to read. This effort by the company demonstrates its confidence in the safety and purity of its product.

You also want to consider the source of the information provided. Such testing should always be conducted by a third party not related to the manufacturer. You also want to verify the certifications of the entity that provided the COA report.

3. What Are the Other Ingredients?

Most CBD topicals on the market contain other additives. Some of the most popular are menthol, camphor, lidocaine, and essential oils. All these additives have the potential to cause a reaction in your clients. Having a basic knowledge of these ingredients can also help you avoid a negative experience when using such products with your clients. Let's get to know a few of the most common additives:

- **Menthol** - a crystalline compound with a cooling, minty odor, found in peppermint and other natural oils. It has analgesic and anesthetic properties and works as a counterirritant and pain reliever. It interacts with TRP receptors to cause a cooling sensation.

- **Camphor** - has analgesic and anesthetic properties. It works as a counterirritant and with TRP pain receptors.

- **Lidocaine -** is a local anesthetic that works by causing temporary numbness/loss of feeling in the skin and mucous membranes.

- **Essential Oils -** are basically plant extracts. They are made by steaming or pressing various parts of a plant (flowers, bark, leaves or fruit) to capture their volatile chemical compounds.

In addition to the additives discussed above, some manufacturers make CBD topicals using additives and dyes which could be harmful. So do your homework: It is essential that you know what you are using with your clients. Make sure you read the labels and avoid CBD products that have synthetic ingredients.

4. Get to Know the Manufacturer

When choosing the CBD product line that you want to carry and use in your massage sessions, you will want to take some time to get to know the company. Read their website and reach out to their customer service department with any questions. Find out if they use a certified Good Manufacturing Practices facility for the production of their products.[15] Look for a brand that offers different levels of their CBD product to accommodate a variety of clients' needs. Different levels can offer access to clients based on different levels of pain and different budgets.

Also it is important to determine the amount of support that you, as a wholesaler, will receive from the company. Look for a company that can offer support with clients' questions about the products, and information about safety and even legal concerns. Also see if they provide useful marketing materials and whether they offer helpful tips on how to grow your business utilizing their products.

Once you choose the company that works best for you, you will want to complete an application to become a wholesaler. This normally requires you to provide basic information about your business and a copy of your sales tax certificate. If you do not have a sales tax certificate (which is a way to verify that no sales tax is due on products that are purchased for resale), you

---

[15] (Good Manufacturing Practices (cGMP) are minimum requirements to ensure that products are created in a manner that ensures they are of consistent quality and safe for their intended use.)

normally can obtain one from your state revenue/ tax department.[16]

After you have been approved as a wholesaler, you can place your first order for product. Most wholesale accounts enjoy pricing that is approximately 50% off the retail price of the product. You will want to clarify if there are any purchase minimums that you will need to make to place an order. Some vendors have timelines in place that require you to place a minimum order within a set time. If you do not meet the qualifications, the vendor/wholesaler relationship will be terminated. Also be aware if there are limitations in the wholesale contract regarding selling the product on certain platforms, such as Amazon, eBay, or Etsy for example. Be sure to read your contract carefully before entering in to the agreement to understand these and any other relevant limitations or restrictions to ensure that they will be suitable based on your plan for sales and use of the product in your service..

---

[16] Normally, the state revenue/tax department's website will outline the process for obtaining such a sales tax certificate. If you are lucky enough to operate your practice in a state without sales tax, this step will be unnecessary.

CHAPTER FIVE

Client and Practitioner Safety

As with every aspect of your practice, the care and safety of your clients must be your first priority. It is also essential that you carefully consider the comfort and safety of the practitioners that work with you in providing the services to your clients. This Chapter will focus on safety considerations for both of those groups when providing CBD massage.

Medications

As with any product used with your clients, you need to be aware of any possible interaction your clients may have, including their use of medications. The way you use CBD, whether orally, sublingually, or topically, contributes to the effect the CBD will have on your clients. This variance stems primarily from the amount of the substance which makes its way into the bloodstream, which varies based on the method of use of the product. For massage therapy, we are only considering the use of CBD administered through the skin with topicals which is the least direct route to the bloodstream. The amount of CBD the body absorbs and sends to the bloodstream through the skin is likely insignificant. Therefore, there is a low probability that your client will experience any sort of interaction with their medication when CBD is applied topically through the use of a lotion or cream. However, it is important to remember as mentioned previously that many CBD products contain additional additives like menthol or camphor. Some of these additives have the potential to cause a reaction in your clients. Thus it is important to discuss all the components of the product with any client before use of the product.

Intake

Having a thorough and documented intake process is a critical part of any practice. The importance of this process is even greater when you are offering additional services to your menu, especially one with the notoriety of CBD. The intake form is a great way for you gather vital data about your client, while also delivering important information about policies and procedures. You have the option of updating your current intake form to include information about CBD add-on products or using a completely different form all together. A good intake form will include all the questions necessary to obtain the information you need from your clients to determine if offering a CBD massage is a safe option for your clients. One key component of the necessary information is a complete list of your clients' medications and current allergies. Instead of just asking your clients if they have any allergies, you may want to be more specific and list some of the ingredients in the product that you have chosen that have a higher risk of skin reaction, like menthol. This reduces the risk for a skin reaction, thus helps to ensure the clients safety.

In addition to your intake form, you should consider including a consent and waiver form related to the use of the CBD product in your intake process. This will provide information to your clients and allow them to make an informed choice about the use of the product. It is also an excellent way to clearly document what was and was not considered and relied upon by the clients in making the decision to agree to the use of a CBD product.

Here is an example of a stand-alone waiver form that may be offered to your clients before their CBD Massage Treatment:

CBD Massage Consent and Waiver

I have read and understand the following:

A Cannabidiol topical product ("CBD") may be used during the massage therapy session. The CBD used in the session has not been approved or endorsed by the FDA or any regulatory agency. The use of CBD is not intended to cure, treat, eliminate, or prevent any disease or medical condition and no claim has been made to me that it will have any such effect. If I have any questions or concerns regarding the use of CBD and its effects on me, I will consult a physician.

The CBD used in the session is derived from hemp and the manufacturer of the product ensures that the product contains no more than 0.3% of THC. Such low levels of THC are non-psychoactive and would be extremely unlikely to trigger a positive drug test.

I had an opportunity to ask questions about the session, the CBD product and this consent and waiver prior to signing. I made an independent decision to participate in the session and agree to the use of the CBD product and I have not relied on the advice of the provider or any of its employees in coming to that decision.

I consent to the treatment, including the use of the CBD product. I assume all risks and liability of participating in the session. I waive, release, and indemnify the provider and its employees from liability for any injury, claim, cause of action, suit, demand, and damages arising in any way from the session, including the use of the CBD product. This waiver includes a claim or action on any basis, including but not limited to, the negligence of the released party and any and all violation(s) of applicable state or Federal law.

Add your signature line, and you are ready to go!

PROACTIVE MASSAGE & BODYWORK
9291 Laurel Grove Road
Mechanicsville, VA 23116
804-559-7990

CBD MASSAGE
Consent and Waiver

Print Name:

Please review and sign at the bottom of the page. (Please ask us if you have any questions, concerns or need additional information):

I have read and understand the following:

A CBD (Cannabidiol) topical product ("CBD") may be used during the massage therapy session. The CBD used in the session has not been approved or endorsed by the FDA or any regulatory agency. The use of CBD is not intended to cure, treat, eliminate or prevent any disease or medical condition and no claim has been made to me that it will have any such effect. If I have any questions or concerns regarding the use of CBD and its effects on me, I will consult a physician.

The CBD used in the session is derived from hemp and the manufacturer of the product ensures that the product contains no more than 0.3% of THC. Such low levels of THC are non-psychoactive and would be extremely unlikely to trigger a positive drug test.

I had an opportunity to ask questions about the session, the CBD product and this consent and waiver prior to signing. I made an independent decision to participate in the session and agree to the use of the CBD product and I have not relied on the advice of the provider or any of its employees in coming to that decision.

I consent to the treatment, including the use of the CBD product. I assume all risks and liability of participating in the session. I waive, release and indemnify the provider and its employees from liability for any injury, claim, cause of action, suit, demand, and damages arising in any way from the session, including the use of the CBD product. This waiver includes a claim or action on any basis, including but not limited to, the negligence of the released party and any and all violation(s) of applicable state or federal law.

Signature: Date:

Therapist Safety

Business owners and therapists often ask if they can get "high" or hurt by absorbing the CBD through their hands and arms while offering multiple massages that incorporates a CBD product. In an effort to respond to this question, remember that in this book, we are only talking about topical CBD cream that has less than 0.3% of THC. Even though CBD topicals with higher levels of THC are legal and available in states where marijuana is legal for recreational use, for this book, we are only referencing CBD topicals from hemp. Because hemp has almost no THC, there is almost no risk that the therapist would experience a psychoactive response. While not conclusive, my personal experience and that of the therapist in my clinic have never reported having any psychoactive effect from consistent, regular use of topical CBD during massage.   In fact, many of the therapists have reported that the contact exposure to CBD in massage sessions has helped them with their own aches and pains.

CHAPTER SIX

Set Up to Sell

In the earliest days of CBD, the sale of the products and use of the products in services were considered high risk to credit card processors thus it could be hard to provide a credit card processor for these products and services. Today finding a credit card processor that accepts payments for CBD is much easier, although you may still find that processors require a higher processing fee to cover the assessed higher risk of CBD products.

Payment Processors

Here are a few of the many processors that will allow CBD sales through their systems:

PaymentCloud - www.paymentcloudinc.com

- Predictable flat-rate pricing

- Month-to-month billing for easy finance tracking

- Excellent customer service

- Extensive compatibility with third-party online shopping carts

Easy Pay Direct - www.easypaydirect.com

- No early termination fee

- Load-balancing feature allows account holders to process higher monthly payments

- High-quality proprietary payment gateway

- Zero complaints on their website

Paywize - www.paywize.com

- Guarantees flat-rate pricing for CBD payment processing

- Compatible with various ecommerce platforms and websites

- Month-to-month billing option

- Broad compatibility with third-party shopping carts

Square – www.squareup.com

- Predictable flat-rate pricing

- No monthly fees

- Very affordable processing hardware

- Suitable for low-volume CBD businesses

Offering Your New Product/Service

So far, we have:

- Learned about CBD and the health benefits it offers.

- Searched the available products lines and chosen the one that best fits within the guidelines you have established for your practice.

- Chosen and set up a merchant account to begin selling your products and services.

- Learned how to protect your clients and your practice with clearly outlined policies and guidelines.

Now let's look at what you need to do to add your new services to your menu.

Step 1 Pricing Your Service

How do you know how much to charge for this new service? There are a few things to keep in mind when determining how much you should charge when adding CBD to your practice. First, you will need to determine how much the product itself is going to cost you. Be sure to include any extra expenses that affect your bottom line like shipping cost, commissions, and use tax before doing the math. When shopping for your product, be sure to ask your supplier if they have back bar sizes. This is a great way to save money by purchasing in bulk. To determine your final cost, you need to break it down. An example of that cost analysis is:

Determining Your Cost
Product:

Mid-Level   High-Level

12 oz $46.50   12 oz $54.00
1 oz =$3.88   1 oz =$4.50
.5 oz =$1.94   .5 oz =$2.25

First let's look at a mid–level oil. Let's say with this product, your cost landed (which includes shipping and use tax) is $46.50 for a 12 oz. bottle. To determine how much an ounce costs, divide $46.50 by 12 which gives you $3.88 an oz. I have found that in my clinic we use 0.5 oz for one add-on service. Assuming that is similar for you, you determine that the cost of 0.5 oz is $1.94. If you are using the higher level oil, the determination would be similar to determine that the cost of 1 oz. would be $4.50. Since we know we only need 0.5 oz. per service, then your cost with the high-level oil add-on would be $2.25 per service.

Determining Your Cost
Supplies:

3 gram container with lid	0.5 oz container with lid	1 oz. container with lid
108/$14.00	125/$13.00	300/$15.00
.10 ea	.13 ea	.05 ea

Next let's look at the cost of supplies. There may be additional costs you need to include other than shipping or tax. If you are trying to control the back-bar supply by distributing pre-measured amounts, then there may be a cost for the containers. You can purchase supply containers in bulk to reduce your cost even more. I use the 1 oz. container which cost $0.05 each.

Once you add up your cost for the container and the product, you can determine your cost per session.

Mid-Level Add-On Cost Per Session

1 oz. container
300/$15.00
.05 ea

4 pumps per session
.5 oz =$1.94

.05 + 1.94 = $1.99 Per Session

In this case, using a 1 oz. container and 0.5 oz. of product and will cost you $1.99 per session. If you charge $15.00 for this add-on service, then your profit will be $13.01. If you have 10 clients choose the CBD add-on to their massage each week that would be an additional $150 of revenue and $130.10 of profits per week. That would be an additional $6,765.20 of profit per year without adding any additional time or expensive equipment costs to your services.

Monthly (4 weeks) Profit Increase

Services	Revenue	Minus Cost	= Profit
40	$600.00	$79.60	$520.40

Annual (52 weeks) Profit Increase

Services	Revenue	Minus Cost	= Profit
520	$7800.00	$1034.80	$6,765.20

You can see how adding this service to your regular menu can be a wonderful opportunity to increase your profits. Keep in mind, most clients will want to purchase the product after they try it, which offers another opportunity for more income.

Now set your goals for how many services you would like to sell per week/month/quarter.

Step 2 Updating Your Service Menu

Decide how you are going to offer CBD in your practice:

- A stand-alone service

- A service add-on

- Retail products for sale

- All of the above!

Stand Alone Service

If you decide to offer CBD massage as a stand-alone service, consider using power words in your service description like:

- pain reduction,

- rapid relief,

- interrupts pain signals,

- calming effect, and

- soothing for your aches and pains.

Here is an example of a full-service description for CBD Massage:

CBD Massage - 30 Min/$65   60Min/$105 90 Min/$135

Each session incorporates CBD massage oils to offer relaxation. Our CBD massage oils combine authorized over-the-counter active pharmaceutical ingredients, with non-psychoactive CBD hemp oil.

These professional massage oils are specially formulated to deliver the pain-relieving OTC compounds directly at the source of discomfort. These powerful counterirritants penetrate deeply through the top layers of the skin with cooling and heating action that interrupts pain signals in the brain allowing you to get the rapid relief you need.

Each massage includes specialty oil spot treatment on problem areas, plus a 3-gram high-level take-home container for self-care.

Be sure to include exactly what the client can expect from this service. For example, will you be spot treating their areas of discomfort, or using a CBD-rich oil all over? For our stand-alone CBD massage in my clinic, we use a mid-level CBD cream to spot treat areas during the massage session. We also include a take home 3-gram container of high-level cream with an information card for self-care.

We do this for two reasons:

1. People love to leave with something they can take home. It adds a lot of client perceived value to the service.

2. It gives clients a chance to fall in love with the product at home. We find they often share it with friends or family who then also come in to pick up a CBD product for their own use. We have a full store in our clinic, so this really helps to boost our overall clinic revenues.

Cost vs. Profit Per Stand-Alone Service

Add $25-$40 upcharge per service
for complete CBD Massage with
take-home product sample

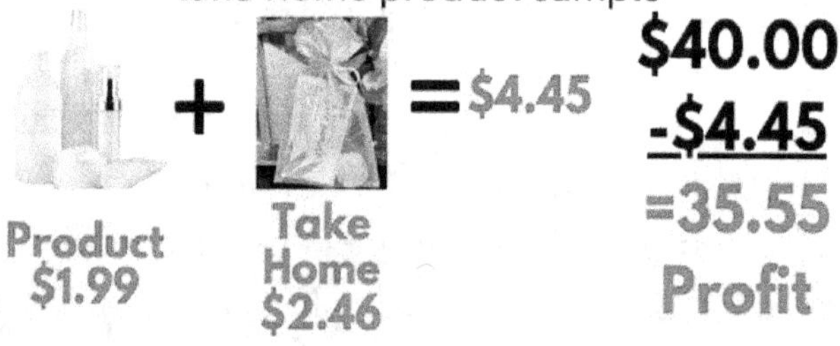

Our costs for the container w/lid, and 3 grams of CBD Cream is $2.46. This take home sample added to the cost of the mid-level product used during the treatment, our total cost for the service is $4.45. We have a $40 up-charge for our complete CBD custom massage service. That is a $35.55 profit on each CBD massage service. Again, let's imagine that 10 clients a week choose this service. That is an additional $400 of revenue and $355.50 of profit per week and an additional $20,800 of revenue and $18,486 of profit per year! As an added bonus, our clients rave about being able to leave with something in hand for home care!

Add-On Option

If an add-on option works for your practice, consider having different levels to meet your clients financial and pain needs. Here is an example of copy to use for your add-on menu and a sample idea of a flyer:

Enrich your session by adding our powerful CBD Massage Oil to your next massage service!

Mid-Level CBD Pain Relief Oil - $10

This powerful mid-level product offers the balance of the active analgesic ingredient (menthol 8%) with therapeutic aromatherapy essential oils and natural emollients for quick absorption. This product is a safe middle ground for anyone seeking strong pain relief but who is not suffering from crippling pain. Includes CBD hemp oil, cottonseed oil, jojoba seed oil, and peppermint oil.

High-Level CBD Pain Relief Oil - $15

The most powerful of the pain relief oils, this oil offers pain relief unleashing the full power of maximum strength menthol (15%) and camphor (5%) in the highest concentrations available on the OTC market. The active ingredients are blended with gentle emollients, including jojoba oil and CBD hemp oil that glides on smoothly to enable powerful pain relief in this revolutionary product.

Once you have created your new service menu, it is time to practice!

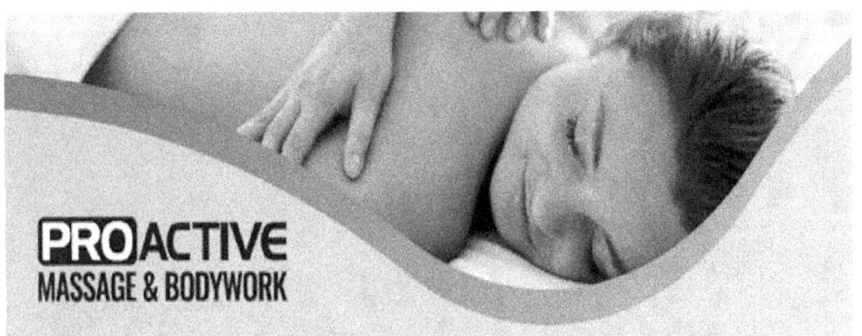

Enrich your session by adding our powerful CBD Massage Oil to your next massage service!

Mid-Level CBD Pain Relief Oil - $10

This powerful mid-level product offers the balance of the active analgesic ingredient (menthol 8%) with therapeutic aromatherapy essential oils and natural emollients for quick absorption. This product is a safe middle ground for anyone seeking strong pain relief but is not suffering from crippling pain. Includes CBD hemp oil, cottonseed oil, jojoba seed oil, peppermint oil.

High-Level CBD Pain Relief Oil - $15

The most powerful of the pain relief oils, this oil offers pain relief unleashing the full power of maximum strength menthol (15%) and camphor (5%) in the highest concentrations available on the OTC market. The active ingredients are blended with gentle emollients, including jojoba oil and CBD hemp oil that glides on smoothly to enable powerful pain relief in this revolutionary product.

f @proactiverva   @proactiverva   ProactiveRVA.com

CHAPTER SEVEN

CBD Massage Protocol

Before offering CBD Massage, it is a good idea to set out a new protocol for your service. Here is a sample protocol for adding CBD Massage into your practice. Be sure to try it out for yourself to test it, and then share it with your staff to prepare them for the new treatment.

What You Need

- CBD Massage Cream or Oil

- 3 Hot Towels

Treatment

Safety Precautions:

1. Always check the temperature of hot towels

to be sure they are at a safe, comfortable temperature level before using them on clients.

2. Never heat CBD Massage Oil in a warmer of any kind.

3. Remember to check in with your clients to be sure they are comfortable during the session.

Session Start: Introduce Touch

While the client is draped, begin introducing touch with palm compression on the back, starting on the mid-back region working towards the low back. Continue walking the hands down the back using compression from the Thoracic region to the top of the pelvis and back up to the top of the shoulders. Decompress the neck and shoulders by applying palms at the top of the shoulders pressing down towards the client's feet.

Warm the Soft Tissues

Undrape the clients back, using proper draping guidelines, and gently place a warm towel over the entire area of the client's back. Walk the hands down the back using compression on top of the warm towel to begin warming the soft tissues.

Apply CBD Oil or Cream

Apply the CBD massage oil or cream to the clients back starting at the lower lumbar region, working up towards the neck and base of the occiput. Repeat the long, gentle glides down the back until the product is evenly distributed. Work the product into the neck and occipital region using bilateral glides up toward the occiput and down toward the proximal edge of the shoulder. Massage the oil in a small, circular motion on the pressure points located at the base of the occiput. Check in with the client to see if the pressure needs to be adjusted before proceeding.

Repeat Protocol

Return to firm glides down the back toward L5 staying along the bilateral sides of the vertebrae connective tissue. Work your way up to the edge of the shoulders, then back in toward the posterior neck muscles then ending at the base of the occiput.

Continue Treatment

Proceed with massage using your custom massage techniques. Be sure the product has been placed on the areas of discomfort as outlined by the client during the intake interview. This will ensure maximum benefit and pain relief.

Closing

Wrap each foot, one at a time, in warm towel compress for approximately 20 seconds. Remove the warm towel and massage the oil onto the unwrapped foot including the joints around the ankles using the techniques of your choice. Repeat steps with a warm towel and massage on the other foot. Finish the session with firm compressions to the toes.

How to bring the products up in session

Even if you do not consider yourself a salesperson, you can find a way to bring CBD products up during a session by simply using your clinical/ therapy skills.

Here are a few tips to try:

- **Try CBD products in session or after a treatment:** You can get direct feedback and buy-in by trying them out with your patients.

- **Show your clients how they work:** Apply a small amount of the cream or oil to the place of pain for the client or show the client where and how to apply it.

- **Offer samples to clients:** Encourage clients to take home a sample of the product to try on themselves and ask for feedback in your next session.

CHAPTER EIGHT

The Big Launch!

A strong marketing plan will help guarantee the success of your new service. Here are a few ideas on how to market your new service:

- Send out an announcement through your email portal to all your customers. Share the exciting news of your updated service menu. In the email, be sure to mention the benefits of CBD and ECS. Consider sharing articles on the benefits of CBD topicals.

- Add a pop-up box on your website offering your new CBD massage service at a discounted introductory rate. Or consider offering a complimentary CBD add-on or take-home sample if they schedule a massage service with you.

- Create a social media countdown to release date. This will build excitement and interest in your new service. During the countdown, offer giveaways, samples, and mentions.

- Create videos of actual client results to share on your website and social media.

- Use subliminal marketing by placing promotional flyers on the doors of treatment rooms and the rest room. Include information about the benefits of CBD cream, especially how it targets pain relief. Don't forget to add a call to action at the bottom of the info flyer.

- Set up an online store. Sell your CBD products direct to customers. Be sure you are using an online store portal that works with CBD suppliers. You will be asked to sign documentation about compliance.

- Have an add-on menu placed in your rest area. Your guests can read about add-on options while they rest and wait for their session to start. Take advantage of having their undivided attention by enticing them with the additional benefits of an add-on service.

- Have samples available for purchase or give-away. Once your clients try your high-quality CBD products, they will be back for more.

- Offer commissions to staff members for sale of products and services. This will benefit both the business and the service provider.

- Train your front desk staff to offer add-ons to clients during the booking process. If product sales are a priority, have them offer a complimentary add-on to get the client to try the product. While there is a slight expense associated with this, your product sales will skyrocket.

- After treatment, offer a Wellness Plan with a recommendation for CBD products. If you have different levels, offer the level that best suits their needs. The next page contains an example of the wellness plan form we give our clients after each session.

These are some great ideas to help you formulate your initial marketing plan. But remember: every successful marketing plan is actually a planning process, not just a onetime plan. It entails regular review and revision.

PROACTIVE
MASSAGE & BODYWORK

9291 Laurel Grove Road | Mechanicsville, VA 23116
804-559-7990 | ProactiveRVA.com

Wellness Plan

Date of Service: _______________________________

Client Name: _______________________________

Exercise: _______________________________

Product:_______________________________

_______Stretch   _______Hydrate   _______Heat   _______Ice

Follow-up Plan

Rebook in:_______________Weeks

Focus On: _______________________________

Therapist: _______________________________

Next Appointment On:_______________________________

Conclusion

As we wrap up our discussion, let's look again at what we covered:

- The basics of the CBD Products.

- ECS.

- The laws and regulations that effect the legality of including the use and sale of CBD in your practice.

- Standards of Practice.

- The factors to consider when choosing a product line.

- Client and practitioner safety.

- How to set up to use and sell CBD products in your practice.

- Establishing a CBD Massage Protocol.

- Creating and implementing your marketing plan.

CBD products can serve as a powerful tool for massage therapists. The growing popularity of hemp extract has everyone wanting to experience the pain-relieving benefits of this powerful product. By adding CBD products to your service menu and your product line, you can fill a need for a pain-relieving option for so many clients while adding incredible profits to your bottom line.

www.ingramcontent.com/pod-product-compliance
Lightning Source LLC
Chambersburg PA
CBHW072037150726
47999CB00002B/962